INVESTIGATE
Alcohol

INVESTIGATE

Marylou Ambrose and
Veronica Deisler

SOUTHERN OAKS

Enslow Publishers, Inc.
40 Industrial Road
Box 398
Berkeley Heights, NJ 07922
USA
http://www.enslow.com

Library of Congress Cataloging-in-Publication Data

Ambrose, Marylou.

   Investigate alcohol / Marylou Ambrose and Veronica Deisler.

      pages cm. — (Investigate drugs)

   Summary: "Find out about the history of alcohol, how it works, its effects, and why people drink"— Provided
   by publisher.

   Includes bibliographical references and index.

   ISBN 978-0-7660-4253-7

   1. Drinking of alcoholic beverages—History—Juvenile literature. 2. Alcoholism—History—Juvenile literature. I. Deisler, Veronica. II. Title.

   HV5020.A56 2015

   362.29209—dc23   2012039703

Future editions:

Paperback ISBN: 978-1-4644-0449-8   EPUB ISBN: 978-4645-1244-2

Single-User PDF ISBN: 978-1-4646-7244-2   Multi-User PDF ISBN: 978-0-7660-5876-7

Printed in the United States of America

052014 Lake Book Manufacturing Inc., Melrose Park, IL

10 9 8 7 6 5 4 3 2 1

To Our Readers: We have done our best to make sure all Internet Addresses in this book were active and ap-
propriate when we went to press. However, the author and the publisher have no control over and assume no
liability for the material available on those Internet sites or on other Web sites they may link to. Any comments
or suggestions can be sent by e-mail to comments@enslow.com or to the address on the back cover.

♻ Enslow Publishers, Inc., is committed to printing our books on recycled paper. The paper in every book
contains 10% to 30% post-consumer waste (PCW). The cover board on the outside of each book contains 100%
PCW. Our goal is to do our part to help young people and the environment too!

Illustration Credits: AP Images/Elise Amendola, p. 9; Centers for Disease Control (CDC)/ Dr. Edwin P.
Ewing, Jr., p. 51; ©Clipart.com, p. 25; ©Digital Stock, p. 47; ©Enslow Publishers, Inc., p. 45; Library of Congress,
p. 32; NASA (National Aeronautics and Space Administration), p. 19 (top); ©Stockbyte Sensitive Issues, p. 5
(bottom); Wikipedia.com Public Domain image, p. 30; Shutterstock.com: (© Alan Poulson Photography, p. 58;
© Andresr, p. 20; © BasPhoto, p. 26; © bayberry, p. 56; © bikeriderlondon, p. 61; © bogdanhoda, p. 38; © Boule,
p. 2; © CREATISTA, p. 85; © iodrakon, p. 90; ©Monkey Business Images, p. 71; ©mountainpix, p. 27; ©Oguz
Aral, p. 13; ©Stephen Finn, p. 87; © yurok, pp. 3, 4, 5 (header), 8, 23, 36, 54, 85, 79, 91–104); © Thinkstock:
(Catherine Yeulet/iStock, p. 70; Fuse, p. 15 (middle left); George Doyle/Stockbyte, p. 17); ©Jason Merrit/
Getty Images Entertainment, p. 19(bottom);© KEMAL BAŞ/iStock, p. 76; ©Kevin Winter/Getty Images
Entertainment, p. 19(middle);© Oleksiy Mark/iStock, p. 15 (middle right); © Palle Christensen/ iStock, p. 15
(bottom); © Paul Vasarhelyi/iStock, p. 83; © Photos.com, p.6;© roxanabalint/iStock, p. 40).

Cover Illustration: Shutterstock.com: © yurok

Contents

Introduction **5**

Chapter 1   **ALCOHOL,** *Seriously*   **8**

Chapter 2   **ALCOHOL** *Through the Ages*   **23**

Chapter 3   **HOW ALCOHOL** *Works*   **36**

Chapter 4   **ALCOHOL'S** *Uncool Aftereffects*   **54**

Chapter 5 — DEALING WITH ALCOHOL *in Everyday Life* — **65**

Chapter 6 — WHAT'S UP *Next?* — **79**

Chapter Notes 91

Glossary 96

For More Information 100

Further Reading and
Internet Addresses. 101

Index 102

Alcohol has been around for a really long time. We know that people made some form of alcohol as long as 12,000 years ago. Since then, alcohol has had its ups and downs. Many people today are still not sure how they feel about it.

So what do you know about alcohol? Did you know it was a drug? Did you know that drinking alcohol moderately has been acceptable in most cultures for thousands of years? Did you also know that drinking too much has been frowned upon for just as long?

On this tomb painting from ancient Egypt ca. 1500 B.C., men can be seen treading grapes to make wine. On the right, men are picking grapes.

Roughly 64 percent of people in the United States drink alcohol. A small number of that 64 percent actually abuse alcohol. They either drink too much over a short period of time or they can't live without it. Unfortunately, the small number who abuse alcohol can affect the rest of us.

This book will give you the straight facts about alcohol. It covers how alcohol works in your body and the many after-effects of using it. It describes the risk factors, symptoms, prevention, and treatment of alcoholism. You'll discover how alcohol can affect a teen's home, school, and social life.

You'll also read stories about real people who've overcome problems with alcohol, and some who weren't so lucky.

You'll get the information you need to make smart decisions about the role alcohol will play in your life, now and in the future.

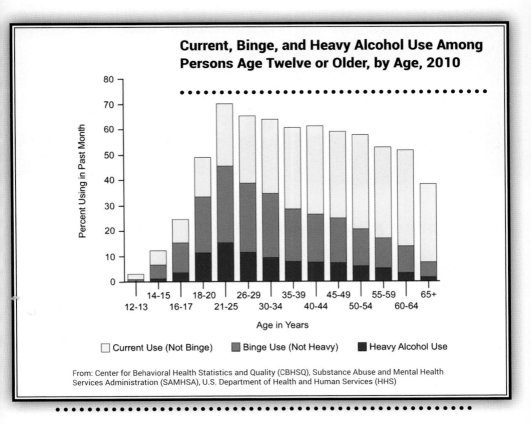

Current, Binge, and Heavy Alcohol Use Among Persons Age Twelve or Older, by Age, 2010

From: Center for Behavioral Health Statistics and Quality (CBHSQ), Substance Abuse and Mental Health Services Administration (SAMHSA), U.S. Department of Health and Human Services (HHS)

In 2010, rates of current alcohol use were 3.1 percent among persons aged 12 or 13, 12.4 percent of persons aged 14 or 15, 24.6 percent of 16 or 17 year olds, 48.9 percent of those aged 18 to 20, and 70.0 percent of 21 to 25 year olds. These estimates were similar to the rates reported in 2009.

Chapter 1

ALCOHOL, Seriously

Stephen King has published more than eighty horror and fantasy books and stories. But the real horror story in his life is how alcohol nearly killed him.

The first time King got drunk was in 1966, during his high school senior class trip to New York City. Back then, the legal drinking age in New York was eighteen, so King was able to buy a bottle of cheap whiskey. He drank most of it himself and was so sick to his stomach, he spent the next day in bed. He missed part of his senior trip and swore he would never drink again. But the next day, he bought a bottle of bourbon and got drunk for the second time.

King continued to drink heavily during his college years at the University of Maine. A month before graduation, he

Novelist Stephen King gestures as he speaks to creative writing students at the University of Massachusetts-Lowell in Lowell, Massachusetts, December, 2012. King struggled with alcoholism for years before becoming sober.

got drunk in a bar and was arrested for driving around and stealing traffic cones. He got off easy, with only a $100 fine.

After college, King became a high school English teacher. He also worked on his writing. Even though he was married and had two young children, he spent his weekends getting drunk. Sometimes he went to bars, but usually, he got drunk at home.

"I found the idea of social drinking ludicrous—if you didn't want to get drunk, why not just have a Coke?" he once said.[1]

King sold his first book, *Carrie*, in 1973. In 1974, he sold *The Shining*. King eventually made enough money from his writing to quit his teaching job. But his drinking only got worse. He was often drunk when he appeared in public to sign his books and was even drunk when he spoke at his mother's funeral! He also began using cocaine and other drugs. He was ashamed and scared, but he couldn't imagine life without alcohol. He was also afraid that if he stopped drinking, he would lose his ability to write. His wife, Tabitha, who is also a writer, would find King passed out in a puddle of vomit next to his desk every morning.

Finally, Tabitha gathered her children, other family members, and friends together at their house. She dumped a trash bag full of her husband's beer cans, cigarette butts, and drugs on the floor. She told him to clean up his act or leave the house for good. It took King a few more years, but with the help of a rehabilitation center and a group called Alcoholics Anonymous, he finally gave up alcohol and drugs in 1989. He's been sober ever since.

Stephen King's family was afraid his drinking would kill him. King himself admits if he hadn't sobered up, he probably would've died years ago.[2] Alcohol might be legal, but its effects on the body can be criminal. Drinking too much can ruin a person's health and also destroy the lives of family members.

Stephen King couldn't imagines a life without using cocaine, drugs, and alcohol.

Straight Facts About Alcohol

Alcohol goes by many slang names: booze, brew, sauce, vino, and a cold one are a few. Types of alcoholic drinks include beer, wine, and hard liquor, such as whiskey, rum, or vodka. Most alcoholic drinks contain fruits or grains. Alcohol is produced when yeast, sugars, and starches are broken down by a chemical process called fermentation.

Alcohol is an unusual substance because it's classified three ways: as a food, a chemical, and a drug. It's a food because it provides energy, or calories. For example, 12 ounces of beer might have 150 calories while 8 ounces of wine could have 200 calories. Alcohol is a chemical because it has a molecular composition. Ethanol, the type of alcohol found in alcoholic beverages, has the chemical composition C_2H_5OH. Alcohol is also classified as a drug of abuse, because it alters consciousness and may be habit-forming.

When a person drinks alcohol, it quickly moves from the stomach and intestines into the bloodstream. There, it travels to every tissue in the body, including those in the brain, liver, and heart. What happens next depends on how much and how fast alcohol is consumed. One or two drinks may make a person feel happy, relaxed, and self-confident. Several drinks will usually cause sleepiness, lack of coordination, slurred speech, and all the signs we associate with intoxication, or drunkenness. If someone drinks a lot of alcohol at one time, he or she can become unconscious or even stop breathing and die.

Drinking too much over a span of time also can be fatal. It can harm the organs and destroy a person's health. For example, alcohol can damage the heart by causing it to

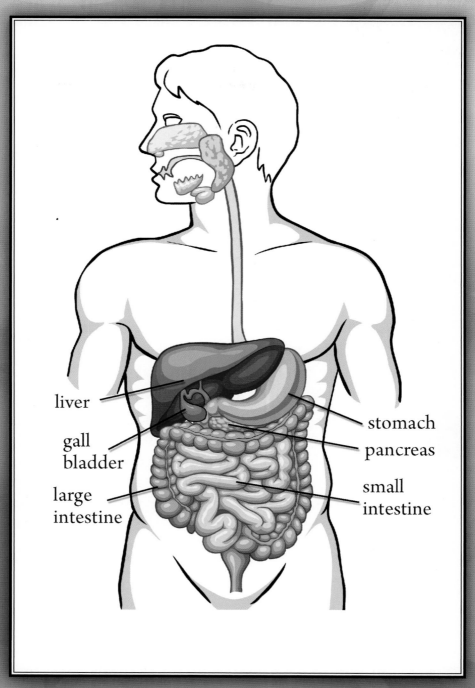

liver

gall
bladder

large
intestine

stomach

pancreas

small
intestine

During digestion, food passes from the mouth into the
stomach and then on to the intestines to be broken down by
digestive juices from the pancreas.

beat irregularly and cause scar tissue to form in the liver and destroy it. Alcohol can even contribute to cancer of the mouth and throat.

How much alcohol is too much? That depends on the person's age, weight, how quickly they drink the alcohol, and many other factors. Many people are responsible drinkers. They have one or two drinks at a party or wedding and never try to get drunk. For them, drinking is something pleasant to do, but it isn't that important in their lives.

For some people, though, no amount of alcohol is safe. Children and teens are in this category. Because their brains are still developing, drinking can have especially dangerous consequences. Pregnant women should also shun alcohol, because drinking can harm an unborn baby. Some people also seem to get hooked on alcohol from their first drink.

Some experts define "heavy drinking" as more than one drink a day for women and more than two drinks a day for men, on a regular basis. One drink is twelve ounces of beer, five ounces of wine, and one-and-a-half ounces of hard liquor. All these drinks contain the same percentage of alcohol.

Alcohol Dependence and Abuse

A person who drinks heavily over a period of time and can't slow down or stop has a disease called alcoholism or alcohol dependence. Alcoholism is a chronic (long-term), progressive disease that can be fatal and may have genetic causes. In other words, some people inherit the tendency to drink excessively.

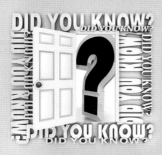
WHAT IS A "Standard" Drink?

In the United States, a standard or average drink is one that contains 0.8 fluid ounces of pure alcohol. The three drinks below are different sizes, but they all contain the same amount of alcohol.

One 12-ounce bottle or can of regular beer (about 5 percent alcohol)

One 5-ounce glass of wine (about 12 percent alcohol)

One 1.5-ounce shot of hard liquor (about 40 percent alcohol)

People with alcohol dependence are called alcoholics and are physically addicted to alcohol. They don't just crave it; their bodies need it. They become sick if they don't get it. This is called alcohol withdrawal. People need more and more alcohol to feel drunk, and they often refuse to admit they have a problem. Many drink even though it wrecks their health, their jobs, and their relationships.

Alcohol abuse is a serious problem, too. It's also known as problem drinking. People who abuse alcohol aren't addicted to it—yet. Even so, they still have plenty of problems caused by heavy drinking, including car accidents, arrests for driving drunk, and trouble at school, work, or home. Long-term problem drinking can eventually lead to alcoholism.

Alcohol abuse and dependency are widespread. Some government sources estimate that about one in six Americans has some type of a drinking problem.[3] Both alcoholics and alcohol abusers may need help from a qualified addiction counselor to get over their problems. Alcoholics may also need to be treated by a medical doctor or hospitalized. Both alcoholics and alcohol abusers can also benefit from attending Alcoholics Anonymous or another support group. (To learn more about support groups, see Chapter 5.)

Underage Drinking

Underage drinking has many risks. Studies show that people who use alcohol before age fifteen are five times more likely to become dependent on it later in life than people who start drinking after age twenty-one.[4] Why? Because

No amount of alcohol is safe for young people.

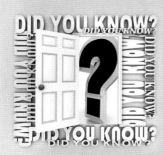

FAMOUS PEOPLE WITH *Alcoholism*

Stephen King is only one of many famous people who are alcoholics. Although some people died, most of the people below were treated and overcame their dependence on alcohol.

Name	Occupation
Edgar Allen Poe (1809–1849)	American mystery/horror writer and poet; died of alcoholism at age forty
Ulysses S. Grant (1822–1885)	18th U.S. president/Civil War general
Ernest Hemingway (1899–1961)	American writer/journalist; committed suicide
Betty Ford (1918–2011)	Wife of President Gerald Ford; founder of Betty Ford Center (for alcohol and drug addiction); died at age 93
Buzz Aldrin (1930–)	American astronaut; second man to walk on moon in 1969
Mickey Mantle (1931–1995)	Yankees baseball player; died of liver disease
Eric Clapton (1945–)	British guitarist/singer/songwriter
Michael J. Fox (1961–)	Canadian-American actor; quit drinking after being diagnosed with Parkinson's disease
Keith Urban (1967–)	American country singer/songwriter
Eminem (1971–)	American rapper/songwriter
Drew Barrymore (1975–)	American actress/child star
Amy Winehouse (1983–2011)	British singer/songwriter; died of alcohol poisoning

Buzz Aldrin
• • • • • • • • • • •

Eminem
• • • • • • • •

Drew Barrymore
• • • • • • • • • • • • •

Many college students admit to drinking alcohol.

the teen brain responds to alcohol differently than the adult brain. This may cause teens to drink larger quantities at one time than adults. This is called binge drinking and is another risk factor for alcohol dependence later on. (To learn more about binge drinking, see Chapter 3.)

When young people, and people of any age, drink on a regular basis, it can actually change or "rewire" their brains—but not in a good way. This may cause problems with memory, coordination, and motor skills that last a lifetime. According to the National Institute on Alcohol Abuse and Alcoholism, each year about 25 percent of college students report the academic consequences of their drinking including missing class, falling behind, doing poorly on exams or papers, and receiving lower grades overall. However, not all people who are heavy drinkers develop these problems. This is because other factors, such as heredity and using other drugs, come into play.

Every year in the United States, 5,000 people under age twenty-one die as a direct result of drinking. They die in car accidents and from alcohol poisoning; they are murdered, commit suicide, drown, and more. At least 190,000 visit hospital emergency rooms because of alcohol-related injuries. Drinking can cause young people to make bad decisions, like engaging in risky sexual behavior, getting in fights, or dropping out of school.[5]

In college, drinking is rampant. About four out of five college students drink alcohol. About half of these are binge drinkers. At least 1,800 students between the ages of eighteen and twenty-four die each year from unintentional

injuries related to alcohol. And 2.8 million admit to drinking and driving.[6]

Alcohol's Effect on Families

Alcohol abuse causes problems for more than just the drinker. Families suffer when a parent or child drinks too much. In families with problem drinkers, adults lose their jobs, mistreat their spouses and children, and push away friends who don't drink. Young people do poorly in school, hang out with other drinkers, and engage in risky behaviors. People of all ages have feelings of shame and fear of abandonment. Marriages often end in divorce. People may also drive when drunk, have accidents, and kill themselves and other people. In 2008, 11,773 people were killed in car crashes involving alcohol. This accounts for nearly one-third of all traffic-related deaths in the United States.[7]

Chapter 2

ALCOHOL
Through the Ages

Alcohol is nothing new. It's been around for thousands of years. It may even go back to the early days of humans. Historians who study artifacts have found ancient beer jugs from the late Stone Age—around 10,000 B.C. They've also found wine jars that go back to 7000 B.C.

How did people create beer and wine so long ago? Was it an accident? No one knows for certain. What we do know is this: Alcohol is made through a simple process called fermentation. It occurs in nature when wild yeast in the air feeds on the sugars in grains, overripe fruits, vegetables, and even honey. Grains turn into beer; fruits become wine. Today's scientists have observed animals and insects who feed on fermented vegetation behave as if they're drunk.

Did you know that yeast is also needed to make bread, which was invented around the same time as beer? In fact, historians aren't sure which came first, bread or beer!

Grapes and Grain Among the Ancients

From the time humans began to live together in villages and cities, clean water was a problem. The rivers that ran through the cities were polluted with human waste products. It was dangerous—even deadly—to drink the water. Beer and wine, on the other hand, were free from pathogens and safe to drink. Pathogens are bacteria and viruses that cause diseases.

If people drank alcohol instead of water, did they get drunk? Not necessarily. Beer and wine had a much lower alcohol content than they do today. You could quench your thirst without major side effects. They also stored very well and could be used as painkillers. Beer and wine were part of everyday life for many ancient cultures. China had its own wine as early as 7000 B.C. It was made with rice, honey, and fruit. The Chinese believed alcohol in moderation was a spiritual food prescribed by heaven. It played a major role in their religious life. The people who lived in the Indus Valley of India from 3000 to 2000 B.C. used an alcoholic drink called Sura. It was made from rice meal. Peasants and warriors especially enjoyed it.

The Sumerians, an ancient farming culture, were the first to write about beer on stone tablets around 3200 B.C. They used it as food, for pleasure, in religious rituals, and as payment for work. The ancient Egyptians used wine and

This limestone figurine (ca. 2350 B.C.) depicts a woman brewer kneading moistened barley dough through a strainer into a large pot, where it would ferment in water.

An ancient Egyptian carving shows two goddesses carrying wine and food offerings to the gods.

beer as medicine. They even stored them in the tombs of pharaohs so they could enjoy them in the afterlife.

The early Greeks first drank mead, a fermented beverage made from honey and water. Around 2000 B.C., they began to grow grapes and make wine, which became an important part of daily meals. They believed that moderate drinking was good for a person's health and happiness. Regular drunkenness was rare, but heavy drinking at banquets and festivals was not unusual. The Romans drank wine moderately, too, but their drinking, over time, became more destructive. By the first century A.D., drunkenness was not uncommon among the upper classes. At the same time, the early Christian Church believed that wine was a gift of God to be enjoyed. You could choose not to drink, but moderate use was okay. Too much drinking, though, was a sin.

This mosaic depicts a Roman picking grapes to make wine.

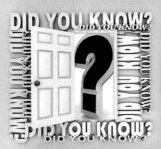

A MODERN DRINKING METHOD
used long ago

Ever wonder where straws came from? The Sumerians and Egyptians drank beer through homemade straws that were hollow reeds. Ancient beer was different from beer today. It was a thick, mildly alcoholic brew that would look more like watery cereal to us. Grain husks, crushed mash from bread, and other remains often floated to the surface. Ancient people used straws to avoid tasting or swallowing the bitter remains while they enjoyed the beer.

The "Water of Life"

During the Middle Ages (500 to 1500 A.D.), vineyards spread across Europe. Christian monasteries began to improve the techniques of making beer and wine. They owned the best vineyards and introduced hops, a dried ripe flower whose oils add a bitter flavor to beer. It also prevents bacteria from causing it to spoil quickly. Beer was a source of nourishment for the monks who had to fast from food for long periods of time. For centuries, the beer and wine they made filled their bellies and supported their lifestyle.

The most important development during this period, though, was distilled alcohol. Distilling is the process of heating a liquid to create a vapor. This is called evaporation. The vapor is then cooled (called condensation) and separated from the original liquid. The cooled vapor is different from the original liquid.

When a fermented drink, such as beer or wine, is distilled, the vapor ends up with a higher alcohol content than in the original liquid. After the steam cools down, you get a stronger drink. The alcohol content of most beers is from 3 to 8 percent. Wines range from 8 to 14 percent. In comparison, most distilled alcohols, such as vodka, whiskey, and rum, are 40 percent alcohol or even higher.

Distilling alcohol wasn't easy. Sometime after the 900s A.D., the Arabs developed a device called the alembic, which simplified the process. The production of distilled alcohol soon traveled to Europe where people noticed this type of alcohol made them feel more relaxed. Some even believed it would help them to live longer. Physicians thought they could also use it as a cure for sickness. They called it "spirit water" or "water of life." At the time, it was actually brandy.[1] Today, we often refer to distilled alcohol as spirits. The word we use most commonly, though, is "alcohol," which comes from an Arabic word that sounds similar.

During the 1300s, distilled alcohol was used for people who suffered from the Black Death, a terrible plague which swept through Europe. It was estimated to have killed almost one third of the population. Alcohol may have eased their pain, but it probably didn't help to keep people alive.

Medieval monks made and drank beer.

Over the centuries, new alcoholic drinks, like vodka, whiskey, rum, and gin, were introduced, but they were mostly used as medicines. After the 1500s, though, social drinking grew in popularity. The sale of alcohol surged, and it became a money-making business. In Britain, gin was distilled in such large quantities that it was cheap, and people consumed a lot of it. In the end, gin was blamed for many health problems and even deaths.

Alcohol Comes to America

When the early colonists left England for America in the 1600s, their ships carried more beer and wine than water. Alcohol was considered safer. Europe's waters were badly polluted during the 1600s and the colonists were afraid that water in the new land would be as dangerous. Also, alcohol kept well on the long sea voyages.

It may come as a surprise that the colonists loved to drink alcohol. In Massachusetts, they cultivated hops and brewed their own beer. Rum, made with molasses shipped in from the West Indies, was also popular among the early settlers. So was hard cider. It was served at meals, and even children drank a weak version of it.

The colonists drank with their meals and while they worked. They also socialized by drinking alcohol. Taverns were the center of activity in most towns. In spite of their love for alcohol, drinking in moderation was an informal rule among the colonists. If you drank too much or too often, you could be whipped or sentenced to hard labor!

Deputy Commissioner John A. Leach of the New York City Police Department (right) looks on as agents pour confiscated liquor into the sewer during Prohibition.

The Rise of Prohibition

During the 1700s and 1800s, the colonies moved from a rural society to an urban one. People no longer had village communities to hold them accountable for drinking too much. As the cities grew, so did poverty, unemployment, and crime. Much of it was blamed on the use of alcohol. Also, attitudes were changing. If you wanted a job in a factory, you needed to be sober. People saw alcohol as a growing social problem.[2]

In 1784, Dr. Benjamin Rush argued that drinking alcohol excessively was bad for your physical and psychological health. Possibly influenced by his ideas, several temperance groups began to form. Temperance means self-control or moderation. At first, the temperance groups recommended moderation in drinking. By 1840, though, they were calling for complete abstinence and a ban of alcohol. They put pressure on politicians and their efforts paid off. In 1920, Congress passed the Eighteenth Amendment, making the manufacture, sale, or transportation of alcohol illegal in the United States. But the amendment didn't work and it was repealed fourteen years later. We call this period Prohibition because to prohibit means to forbid something.

A New Theory

It was clear that banning alcohol didn't work. But how could you help people who drank too much? Society's ideas were about to change. Until now, drunkenness had been considered a moral weakness. Drinking too much showed a lack of willpower. But a new idea emerged in the 1800s. Perhaps drinking too much alcohol was an illness.

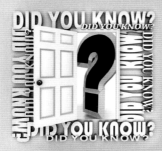

WHEN DRINKING WAS *Against the Law*

From 1920 to 1933, making or selling alcohol was illegal in the United States. Those who liked the new law called it "The Noble Experiment." But not everyone thought it was a great or noble idea. Many Americans were angry that their right to drink alcohol had been taken away. People who sold or made alcohol for a living were especially upset, because it put them out of business.

Enforcing the law was almost impossible. Alcohol was smuggled into the United States across the Canadian border or from Europe on ships. People brewed liquor in secret. Illegal bars known as "speakeasies" cropped up all over the country. Unlawful liquor manufacturers, known as "bootleggers," prospered. They even bribed the police and other public officials to look the other way. It was the age of gangsters, and many movies have wrongly glamorized this time period.

The Noble Experiment failed. It had actually caused people to drink more and commit more crimes!

Back in 1784, Dr. Benjamin Rush had suggested that having no control over alcohol was a sickness. Then, in 1849, a Swedish doctor coined the term "alcoholism." But it wasn't until 1959 that the American Medical Association (AMA) officially classified alcoholism as a disease. Today there are many programs available that help people who have an addiction to alcohol. An addiction is a constant, uncontrollable need for a substance, even though the user knows it's harmful.

Then and Now

For centuries, alcohol has played an important role in almost every culture. From the earliest times, it was valued as a food, a refreshing drink, and a medicine. It also played a large role in religion and provided a vital source of income. Plus, alcohol has improved the quality of life for many people.

Most cultures have believed, and still believe, that moderate drinking is acceptable. At the same time, alcohol abuse has always existed. People have tried to find ways to stop it but haven't succeeded.

Today's attitudes toward alcohol vary. Most people can enjoy a drink or two without abusing it. Religious groups, such as Muslims and some Buddhists, forbid its use. Some people are addicted to alcohol. Once they start, they can't seem to stop. Many of them have ruined their lives because of an addiction.

One thing is clear: Alcohol will continue to play a significant role in countries and cultures around the world.

Chapter 3

HOW ALCOHOL *works*

Julia Gonzalez, age sixteen, was a typical teenager. She liked to hang out with friends and talk on her cell phone. She also liked to drink. At least she did on the night of December 29, 2008, when her grandmother saw her climb into a car with three other people. That was the last time she saw Julia alive.

At 5 A.M. on December 30, a passerby found Julia's lifeless body in a park three miles from her home in Turlock, California. An autopsy revealed a shocking fact: Julia's blood-alcohol concentration (BAC) was 0.52 percent. This is six-and-a-half times the legal limit for intoxication in California. At only 5 feet 2 inches tall and 100 pounds, Julia would have had to drink the equivalent of sixteen drinks in one hour to register that high. The cause of death? Alcohol poisoning from binge drinking.

The doctors said that at first, Julia would have seemed very, very drunk. Then she probably lost consciousness and stopped breathing, or her heart stopped pumping, or both. If her friends had called 911 when they noticed how sick she was, Julia might be alive today.

What happened to the friends Julia left home with? Were they with her when she got drunk and passed out? Were they afraid to call the ambulance because they didn't want to get caught drinking illegally? Did they know Julia was dead when they left her in the park? There are many unanswered questions.

"We can't find anyone willing to say they were in Julia's company while she was consuming alcohol or intoxicated," Turlock Police Detective Brandon Bertram said during the investigation.[1]

No one ever came forward. To this day, Julia's family doesn't know exactly what happened. They know Julia drank enough to kill her. But they may never know why her friends didn't call for help or how Julia ended up in the park. The police ruled the death accidental and closed the case after three months.[2]

What happened to Julia is a tragedy. The fact that her friends didn't help her makes it sadder still. Possibly, they didn't realize how sick she was until it was too late, and then they panicked. Or they might have thought she would "sleep it off" and be fine, not realizing she was actually in a deep, unconscious state called a coma.

Julia died from alcohol poisoning. She would have had to drink the equivalent of sixteen drinks in one hour to become this intoxicated.

• •

People who have consumed as much alcohol as Julia did aren't asleep, they're unconscious. They can't "sleep it off." This is one of many mistaken beliefs about alcohol held by people of all ages, not just young people. This chapter will expose some common myths about alcohol, describe how alcohol affects your body, and reveal the problems that can occur when people drink wine, beer, and spirits.

The Lure of Alcohol

Everyone has seen ads for alcohol on TV and thought, "Wow! Those guys are having an awesome time!" Advertisers spend millions every year to make their products look glamorous and fun. Ads for alcohol are everywhere. There are even mobile phone apps for different brands of alcohol. Many movies aimed at teens revolve around trying to score alcohol and the "hilarious" consequences of getting drunk.

In other words, images of alcohol are everywhere, and everyone is influenced by them. Teens may think that drinking is the best way to fit in, make friends, feel cool, or chill out. If so many people on TV are drinking, it must be harmless, right? Sometimes, sometimes not.

This Is Your Body on Alcohol

What happens in a person's body after he takes a drink? Alcohol passes from the mouth, down the esophagus, and into the stomach. A small amount passes into the bloodstream through the stomach, but most travels into the small intestine. Then it passes through the intestinal walls into the bloodstream. After that, the heart pumps the alcohol throughout the body, to the brain, liver, heart, kidneys, lungs, and other organs and tissues.

Alcohol mixes with water in the blood and body tissues and becomes diluted, or weaker. Once it's absorbed into the tissues, the alcohol exits the body through the kidneys, lungs, and liver. Five percent of the alcohol is eliminated in urine, and 5 percent is exhaled by the lungs. The remaining 90 percent is changed into water, carbon dioxide, and energy by the liver. This process is called oxidation.

The liver removes the alcohol from the blood to prevent damage to the cells and organs. This happens slowly, at a rate of about 0.5 ounces of alcohol per hour. But if someone drinks too much too fast, the alcohol builds up in the body and the person gets drunk.

Alcohol ads appear on many social media sites.

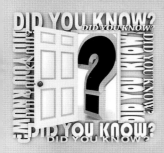

ALCOHOL CAN *Kill*

Alcohol can poison you if you binge drink—drink too much in a short period of time. That's what happened to Julia Gonzalez. How does your body react? Violent vomiting is usually the first sign. People may also get confused, have trouble breathing, have seizures, and pass out. Without medical help, they can have permanent brain damage. Or, they can die if they stop breathing or inhale vomit into their lungs. If you notice any of these problems in a friend who's been drinking, call 911 immediately!

In the United States, binge drinking is defined as consuming five or more drinks in a row by men. For women, it's four or more drinks in a row. Those amounts will bring a person's BAC to 0.08 percent or above. Heavy binge drinking is defined as three or more occurrences within a two-week period.

About 15 percent of adults admit to binge drinking. The number may be even higher, since people often say they drink less than they actually do. Binge drinking is a major problem among underage drinkers. Even though drinking alcohol is illegal for them, people aged twelve to twenty drink 11 percent of the alcohol consumed in the United States. More than 90 percent of it is consumed during binge drinking![3]

During oxidation, the body produces a by-product of alcohol called acetaldehyde. This is a poison. Acetaldehyde affects the central nervous system, causing slurred speech, loss of balance, and all the signs of drunkenness. People think a drunk is funny, but they wouldn't if they knew the person was actually being poisoned. When people vomit after drinking too much, this is the body's way of getting rid of the poison.

Blood alcohol concentration, or BAC, is the amount of alcohol present in a person's blood after drinking. It's also called blood alcohol content or blood alcohol level and is measured as a percentage. Someone who has a BAC of 0.08 percent has 8 grams of alcohol for every 100 milliliters of blood. This is the legal limit for driving in all states.

How People Act on Alcohol

People who are drinking look, act, and feel in typical ways. However, alcohol doesn't affect everyone the same way. It depends on how much they drink, how fast they drink, and other factors. For example, if people drink on an empty stomach, alcohol passes into the bloodstream more quickly and they get drunk faster. Mixing alcohol with carbonated drinks is popular with young people. But this also causes alcohol to be absorbed into the bloodstream faster. In addition, the less a person weighs, the less blood and body water they have to absorb the alcohol. So people who are heavier can drink more without getting drunk.

In spite of these differences, everyone's body reacts to alcohol gradually. Below are the stages of intoxication:

Euphoria:

People feel relaxed and self-confident. They become talkative and say things they wouldn't normally say. Their faces may become flushed, and their judgment and coordination may not be good. This is a result of the person being poisoned by alcohol, until the body can eliminate it.

Excitement:

People have poor coordination and balance, slow reaction time, and drowsiness. They usually believe they're functioning better than they are.

Confusion:

People have trouble walking, blurry vision, and slurred speech. They may be overly emotional, laughing, crying, or being affectionate.

Stupor:

People can't stand or walk, they vomit, and they become unresponsive. They may pass out.

Coma:

People are unconscious, their body temperature is below normal, their breathing is shallow, and their heart rate slows down. They may die.

Death:

People stop breathing and die. The higher the BAC, the greater the chance of death. A BAC of .41 or greater leads to death.

Responsible Drinking

Is drinking alcohol something to avoid at all costs? Not usually. Many adults drink responsibly. Enjoying a glass of wine with dinner, having a beer at a baseball game, or sipping a drink at a party can be relaxing, fun, and help adults feel more at ease. Wine is especially popular among adults.

They often enjoy learning about it, collecting different brands, and even making it at home.

When young people drink, it's a different story. Most don't drink to relax; they drink to get drunk. Some binge drink. Drinking becomes an experiment, a way to fit in, or a challenge. This kind of drinking causes big problems: car accidents, losing your license, getting kicked off sports teams, and maybe even getting killed. Young people rarely are responsible drinkers.

What is responsible drinking? It's drinking in a safe, legal manner, without aiming to get drunk. Responsible drinkers don't drink a lot in a short period of time and don't drink shots or play drinking games. They're informed drinkers who are aware of their body's rate of eliminating alcohol, so they set limits on how much they'll drink. They don't let other people's drinking behaviors influence how much they drink. And they don't let their drinking patterns harm themselves or others.

Responsible drinkers avoid drinking and driving. Research shows there's probably no safe amount of alcohol to drink before driving. Responsible drinkers know that some impairment may occur even with one or two drinks. So they appoint a "designated driver." This is someone who doesn't drink at all on that occasion and drives the people who are drinking home.

What Causes Alcohol Problems?

Why is alcohol a problem for some people but not others? How come some people are content with having one beer, while others have to pound down the whole six-pack?

Effects of drinking for a 140-pound woman	Blood Alcohol Content
Attention may decrease	.01
Reaction time slows	.02
Tracking and steering affected	.03
Vision impaired	.04
Coordination decreases	.05
Judgment impacted	.06
	.07
Legal limit; hard to concentrate or control speed	.08
Marked loss of coordination and judgment	.09
	.10

Several factors increase a person's risk of becoming a problem drinker, including the following:

Genes:

Scientists have discovered several genes linked to alcoholism, including one related to binge drinking in young people. So some people are born with a tendency toward alcohol abuse.

Family history:

Alcohol problems seem to run in some families. Children of alcoholics have a higher risk of becoming alcoholics, too. Plus, if drinking is acceptable in a family, children will consider this normal behavior.

Gender:

More men than women are heavy drinkers

Mental Health:

People who are depressed, anxious, or have other emotional problems are more likely to abuse alcohol to try to make themselves feel better. Children with attention deficit hyperactivity disorder (ADHD) and impulsive, aggressive, or antisocial behavior are also at risk for problem drinking.

Drinking patterns:

People who regularly drink too much for an extended time period may become dependent on alcohol.

Social factors:

Having friends who drink a lot increases a person's chance of becoming a problem drinker, too.

Drinking and driving do not mix. Do not get into any car with a person who has been drinking. Your decision not to could save your life.

• •

Cultural factors:

Seeing heavy drinking portrayed as glamorous and fun on TV, in movies, and in social media makes people think drinking too much is okay.

Child abuse:

Children who were abused are more apt to become problem drinkers later in life.

Signs of Alcohol Dependence or Abuse

Some alcoholics or alcohol abusers are in denial. Others may be aware they have a problem but aren't ready to take the first steps to get help. Or they may feel powerless to stop drinking. How can you tell if a friend or family member needs help for an alcohol problem? Look for one or more of the following signs:

- They keep drinking even when their job, schoolwork, relationships, or health are falling apart.

- They try to hide the amount they're drinking from others, or minimize it. They get aggressive and physical when drinking.

- They get mad when you say they drink too much.

- They need to drink to get through the day.

- They stop eating properly.

- They stop caring how they look or even if they're clean.

- They shake if they haven't had a drink in several hours.

- They can't remember what they did while drinking. They may even have memory lapses when they aren't drinking. For instance, they might drive past their exit on the highway and suddenly wonder where they are.

- They need more and more alcohol to get drunk.

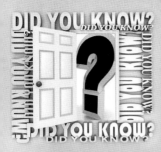

ALCOHOL AND
Ethnic Groups

Some ethnic groups tolerate alcohol better than others. Why? Both genes and culture play a part.

Americans of European descent usually tolerate alcohol well because they've had thousands of years to get used to it. Europeans were drinking wine back in 2000 B.C.! Over the centuries, their genes adapted and their bodies acquired high levels of the enzyme alcohol dehydrogenase. This enzyme helps the body metabolize and then get rid of acetaldehyde, the poison found in alcohol. It's all part of the evolutionary process.

This isn't true for people of Asian descent. Some of them have a genetic mutation that causes their bodies to turn alcohol into acetaldehyde much faster. So when they drink, their faces get red, they sweat, their body temperature rises, their heart rate goes up, and they feel sick to their stomach. This is called "Asian flush," and is the body's attempt to get rid of the poison. Because of this reaction, many Asians avoid alcohol.

Native Americans have a reputation for not being able to tolerate alcohol. Although alcoholism is high within this ethnic group, genes may not be the only reason. Poverty, unemployment, lack of education, low self-esteem among young people, and loss of the Indian way of life are probably more to blame. Also, Native Americans were introduced to alcohol fairly recently in history—in the mid-1600s. So compared to Europeans, their genes haven't had as much time to change and develop a tolerance to alcohol.

Stages of Alcoholism

People don't become alcoholics overnight. It can take up to fifteen years to go from the early stage of alcoholism to the final stage. People must get professional help early, before the disease does permanent physical harm or even kills them.

Early Stage

This is also called the adaptive stage. Drinking stops being a social activity. People drink to escape from their problems and make themselves feel better. Their tolerance increases, and they can drink more than their friends without getting drunk. They usually don't appear to have a drinking problem.

Middle Stage

This is also called the dependence stage. The body gets used to higher amounts of alcohol and needs it to function. People plan their schedules around drinking, may start drinking earlier in the day, and then may not be able to stop. They have blackouts and hangovers. When they can't get alcohol, they have withdrawal symptoms, such as sweating, anxiety, shaking, and hallucinations. Their lives unravel, and they have trouble at work, at school, and at home. Everyone notices they have a drinking problem.

Final Stage

This is also called the endstage. The body has been poisoned over the years, and serious physical problems occur. People develop heart disease, liver disease, malnutrition, mental confusion, and brain damage. They lose their jobs, have financial problems, and drive away friends and family. Drinking becomes the main focus of their lives, and nothing else matters. They ignore basic needs like food, shelter, and personal hygiene. The only way to get off alcohol at this stage is with immediate medical help. People must be hospitalized to go through withdrawal. If they try to quit on their own, they can die from delirium tremens, severe withdrawal that includes hallucinations and seizures. Even with medical help, the alcoholic may suffer permanent physical damage that ruins his health and shortens his life.

Myths about Alcohol

People have many false impressions about alcohol. Here are some of the most common myths.

- Getting drunk kills brain cells. Alcoholics, however, can develop a disorder that destroys the nerve cells in the brain. It causes memory loss, confusion, loss of coordination, and even death.

• •

During an autopsy, this brain of an alcoholic was found to be inflamed. Drinking can cause permanent brain damage.

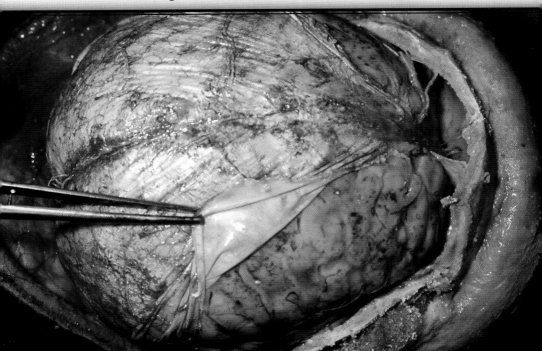

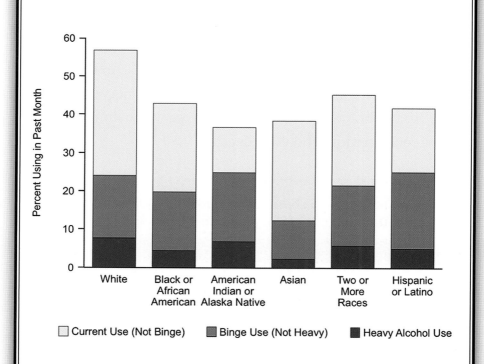

Current, Binge, and Heavy Alcohol Use among Persons Age Twelve or Older, by Race/Ethnicity, 2010

Center for Behavioral Health Statistics and Quality (CBHSQ), Substance Abuse and Mental Health Services Administration (SAMHSA), U.S. Department of Health and Human Services (HHS)

- Drinking causes a "beer belly." Consuming too many calories causes a big belly. Overweight people may get some extra calories from alcohol, but they also eat too much food. They may also snack when they drink, because alcohol can increase your appetite.

- Coffee sobers you up. Nope. Cold showers and "walking it off" don't help, either. Only time can sober you up.

- Wine is good to drink because it has less alcohol. Wine might taste "lighter" than beer, but a 5-ounce glass has the same alcohol content as a 12-ounce bottle of beer. Both have the same alcohol content as 1.5 ounces of spirits.

- People who can "hold their liquor" are lucky. Actually, people who can drink heavily without getting drunk have built up a tolerance for alcohol. They have to drink more and more to feel a buzz and may be on the road to becoming alcoholics. Also, being able to hold your liquor is a sign you may have a genetic risk for alcoholism.

- Everyone drinks in this country. Not true. The United States is number thirty-two on the list of alcohol-consuming countries.

Chapter 4

ALCOHOL'S
Uncool Aftereffects

Tyler,* a high school senior, was invited to a party given by Sarah,* a girl in his class. Sarah and her family lived in a private community with strict rules and its own security patrol. The party was supposed to be at her house. But when Tyler arrived, Sarah's parents told him the kids were down at the lakeshore.

When Tyler arrived at the lake, the party was in full swing. At least two dozen teens were drinking beer, and open containers were everywhere. Tyler had nothing against drinking. In fact, he'd arrived expecting alcohol to be served. He'd planned to crash at Sarah's house or even sleep in his car, rather than drink and drive. He knew about the community's strict rules, and the lakeside party looked

* Not their real names

like a bad scene to him. He decided to stick around but not drink, just in case.

Tyler looked for a place to park his car, but the only spot close-by was in someone's driveway. "The house was all dark, and I saw a snow shovel leaning against the garage," he said. "It was May, and I figured they were summer people who hadn't been there in a long time." So he decided it was okay to park in the driveway.

Within minutes of arriving back at the party, Tyler saw a patrol car pull up with its lights flashing. Kids scattered everywhere, throwing their beer cans and running into the woods. Tyler thought about running but decided not to. After all, he wasn't doing anything wrong.

The security patrolman didn't agree. He didn't even bother chasing the other kids. He just told Tyler to get in the car, because he was in big trouble. Tyler said, "I wasn't drinking," but it didn't matter. When the patrolman asked if that was Tyler's car parked in someone's driveway, Tyler said yes. The patrolman told him he was in even more trouble for trespassing.

Back at headquarters, the patrolman called the state troopers. The troopers arrived and had Tyler take a breathalyzer test to check for alcohol. He had no alcohol in his blood. He didn't get in trouble with the state police, but the community slapped him with hundreds of dollars in fines. On top of this, Tyler's car was impounded—towed to a locked lot—and his parents had to pay $250 to get it out. They weren't happy and neither was Tyler. That car was his prized possession, and he worried that it might've been damaged by the tow truck.

A breathalyzer measures a person's blood alcohol content.

Luckily, the car got through okay, and so did Tyler. But he learned a lesson: When alcohol is involved, you can get punished just for being in the wrong place at the wrong time. He knew enough not to drink and drive, but just being at an underage drinking party can get you in trouble. What about the other kids who ran off? None of them had to pay fines, but some of them probably drove home drunk that night. Luckily, no one was in an accident.

As for Sarah's parents, they were smart not to host a teenage drinking party at their home. But they were foolish to let Sarah have an unsupervised party somewhere else in the community. In the end, they had to pay fines, too, when the community police found out their daughter had given a party in a public area where no after-hours partying was allowed.[1]

As Tyler's story shows, alcohol can get you into trouble even when you aren't drinking it. When you are, it can get you into worse trouble. Driving while drunk or impaired can cause a person to lose his or her license or even go to jail. Adults who host underage drinking parties can also face severe penalties.

Drinking and Driving

According to the National Highway Traffic Administration, more than 10,000 people died in 2010 from car crashes involving alcohol. That adds up to one person every fifty-one minutes.[2] No wonder states have tough laws when it comes to driving under the influence of alcohol!

In all fifty states, 0.08 percent is the maximum blood alcohol concentration (BAC) a person twenty-one or older can have and still legally drive. For drivers who are not of legal drinking age, the BAC limit is even lower—zero in many states. Punishments for driving while impaired or drunk differ from state to state, or even county to county. They also differ depending on whether the driver is a first offender or has had other driving under the influence (DUI) arrests. The more previous arrests, the stiffer the penalties are. For example, people who've have three DUIs often get sentenced to five years in jail and lose their license forever.

You don't have to be drunk to get in trouble with the law. You just have to have a blood alcohol concentration higher than the legal limit. Penalties for a first offense may include losing your license for at least six months or paying a fine of several hundred dollars or more. You may also have to do community service, like picking up roadside

trash. Jail time is also possible. Many states also make a person attend alcohol education classes.

In addition, people arrested for driving under the influence may have their cars impounded and have to pay stiff fines to get them back. They also have to pay a lot for car insurance, as well as pay lawyers. If they had a car accident and someone else was hurt, the victim or the victim's family may sue them. People with DUI convictions may have trouble finding work because they have a criminal record. Or they may lose their job because they have no way to get there without a license. They can also never get a job that involves driving, such as driving a tractor trailer or a delivery van.

Driving with open bottles of alcohol is a crime in many states.

Driving with an open container of alcohol is also a crime in many states. Some states allow passengers to drink alcohol. Other states don't allow a bottle, can, or container of alcohol to be anywhere in the car.

Sobriety Tests

Suppose someone who's had a few too many beers gets stopped by the police. What happens next? And how do the police tell whether the driver has a BAC above the legal limit?

There are several reasons someone might get pulled over and tested for alcohol. A driver might be weaving all over the road. Or he or she might get stopped for something as simple as a broken tail light. In any case, if the officer smells alcohol or sees an open container, he'll test the driver for intoxication.

Another way to get stopped is at a sobriety checkpoint. The police usually set up checkpoints late at night, on weekends, or on holidays. Places with heavy traffic are favorite sites, such as exit points of concerts or football games. Most states allow these checkpoints, but they're illegal in eleven states. Studies show that sobriety checkpoints reduce alcohol-related accidents by about 20 percent.[3]

Let's say a driver gets stopped at a sobriety checkpoint and the police officer smells alcohol on his breath. Now what? The officer will ask the driver to perform some field sobriety tests. Failing these tests gives the police good cause to arrest a person.

Field sobriety tests require a person to follow orders and perform simple physical tasks. For example, the officer may shine a small flashlight into the driver's eyes, move it from side to side, and ask the driver to follow the light. If the eyes jerk a lot or the driver can't follow the light smoothly, he or she is probably impaired.

In another test, a driver gets out of the car and walks nine steps along a straight line, and then turns and walks back the same way. A third common test requires a driver to stand on one foot. People who can't keep their balance or follow directions in these two tests are probably impaired.

The police officer may also ask the driver to blow into a breath alcohol testing instrument. This device measures the amount of alcohol in the blood. Refusing to take this test is a bad idea. Even people who are completely sober will immediately lose their license for up to a year. If they aren't sober and are later convicted of drunk driving, their licenses are taken away for even more time.

In many states, the police can also transport a driver to the hospital and have a blood test performed to measure BAC. This usually happens when an accident occurs or with people who've had DUI convictions before.

Testing for Alcoholism

There are no blood tests just for alcoholism, and it can't be diagnosed by an X-ray. The blood tests or breath tests done to measure BAC only show if someone has alcohol in their blood. They can't reveal if a person is actually an alcoholic.

So how does a doctor decide if a person is a problem drinker? Most likely, they'll ask questions or have the

An officer will check a person's ability to do simple physical tasks during a field sobriety test.

• •

patient fill out a survey. Some surveys contain only a few questions, while others have up to twenty-five questions. These simple tests are quite accurate, as long as the patient tells the truth. Unfortunately, people may lie or underestimate the amount they actually drink.

The Rutgers Alcohol Problem Index is a test used to assess problem drinking in young people. You complete a twenty-three-item survey by circling how many times certain things happened to you while drinking or because of drinking in the past year. Some items include "Went to work or school high or drunk," "Caused shame or embarrassment to someone," and "Wanted to stop drinking but couldn't." A high score indicates problem drinking.

If a doctor has cared for a patient a long time, he'll notice changes in the person's health that may be caused

by alcohol. He will then help the patient get treatment. The doctor may do a blood test to see if the patient's liver is damaged from alcohol. Finding out they have liver damage convinces some people to seek treatment for alcoholism.

Health Problems from Alcohol Abuse

Heavy drinking over a long period of time can cause serious health problems. Here are some common ones:

Liver disease: Heavy drinking can eventually destroy the liver, causing a disease called cirrhosis. Destruction halts if a person stops drinking, but he or she might die without a liver transplant.

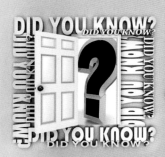

GIVING ALCOHOL to Minors

Knowingly supplying alcohol to minors is illegal in every state. It's illegal for bars and restaurants to serve people under age twenty-one. It's illegal for parents to hold underage drinking parties at their homes. And it's illegal for twenty-one year old college students to buy beer for younger students. Penalties include fines of up to thousands of dollars and jail time up to five years. People may also go on probation, which means they have to report to an officer of the court on a regular basis. Stiffer penalties are given if a minor is injured or dies after drinking alcohol provided by an adult. Bar or restaurant owners face the same penalties, as well as higher fines and the loss of their liquor licenses.

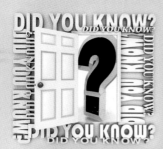

BABIES AND ALCOHOL
Don't Mix

Fetal alcohol syndrome is a serious problem for babies of alcoholic women. When alcohol passes through the placenta to the fetus, it can cause harm. Infants born with fetal alcohol syndrome can have a number of symptoms: slow growth, delayed development, poor coordination, learning disabilities, and heart, bone, and kidney defects.

Although drinking any time during pregnancy isn't recommended, drinking during the first three months seems to be the most harmful. There is no safe level of alcohol when you're pregnant. Binge drinking is especially damaging to an unborn baby. The greater the amount of alcohol, the greater the damage to the fetus.

Digestive problems: Drinking too much can cause gastritis, an irritation of the stomach lining. It can also damage the pancreas, an organ that helps with food digestion.

Heart trouble: Heavy drinking can lead to high blood pressure and a weak heart muscle that can't pump enough blood to the organs. It can also cause a stroke—a blood clot that keeps blood from reaching the brain.

Sexual problems: Men can have trouble getting an erection if they drink too much. Women can stop getting their periods.

Immune system problems: Too much drinking can make it harder for the body to fight off diseases.

Bone loss: Excessive alcohol use can lead to brittle bones and fractures.

Nerve problems: Heavy drinking can cause the hands and feet to go numb and cause memory problems.

Cancer: Excessive alcohol use can make people more apt to get mouth, throat, colon, liver, and breast cancer.

Birth defects: Women who drink while pregnant may have babies with fetal alcohol syndrome. This disease causes mental retardation and growth problems.

Chapter 5

DEALING WITH ALCOHOL

in Everyday LIfe

Doug* is sixteen and has never seen his father drink alcohol. But his mother Linda* has. On their first date, her ex-husband bragged about never getting a ticket for a DUI, even though he'd been stopped at several roadblocks after drinking alcohol.

Linda thought nothing about it. The man she eventually married didn't fit her image of an alcoholic. He was smart, had graduated from an Ivy League school, and was very successful in his career. When they went out drinking with friends, he was always joking and jovial—the life of the party. After the parties, however, the joking stopped. If her husband didn't pass out, he would become mean and nasty. The next day he would apologize and promise never to drink too much again.

* Not their real names

Linda's husband didn't drink every day. He often gave up alcohol for periods of time, but he always went back. The marriage was falling apart, so the couple went for counseling. When the counselor suggested they go to an Alcoholics Anonymous (AA) meeting, Linda agreed, if only to prove her husband wasn't an alcoholic. Instead they came across an Al-Anon meeting—a support group for family and friends of problem drinkers. It was at that meeting that Linda realized that her husband fit the description of an alcoholic.

Linda's husband joined AA and became sober. The couple soon had children, including Doug. But Linda learned that quitting alcohol was only part of the healing process. Meetings were also needed to keep the emotional issues that go along with alcoholism under control.

"When my husband went to meetings regularly, his behavior with the family was good," said Linda. "When he missed meetings because of work or for other reasons, his attitude changed. He got angry easily, started hitting Doug, and went into a depression. He even hit me once."

Eventually, Linda asked for a divorce. Her husband lashed out at her and fought for full custody of the children.

"He said that if I didn't stay in the marriage, he would make me pay for it," Linda said.

The two now share joint custody of their children. Although Linda's husband says he no longer drinks, he has stopped going to AA meetings.

"When he was going to AA, my dad was a happy person," Doug said. "Now he seems angry all the time. Once he pushed me up against the wall and almost put me through it!" Doug's dad doesn't see himself as an angry person.

"Why don't you go back to AA?" Doug has asked his father. "When you go to a doctor or get help, you're better."

"I don't drink anymore, so I don't need to go," his father answered.

Doug started to get help from Alateen (a support group for young people who live with an alcoholic) when he was thirteen. It was a no-brainer. "I saw my mom was a calm,

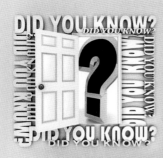

WHAT'S A "Dry Drunk"?

Alcoholics can develop many unpleasant behaviors while they're drinking. When an alcoholic is in recovery, those behaviors don't disappear. Someone who keeps up those behaviors is called a "dry drunk." Friends and family may be so used to the way they act that they don't even realize there's still a problem. For example, Doug's father in the story stopped drinking, but he continued to use his family as a punching bag for his problems.

Recovering alcoholics can be resentful, frustrated, jealous of others, afraid of failure, and ashamed of time wasted being drunk. If not dealt with, those feelings can explode. There is hope, however. A professional substance abuse counselor or a twelve-step program, such as Alcoholics Anonymous, can help recovering alcoholics work through their problems so that they can feel good about themselves again.[2] A twelve-step program is a set of guiding principles that outline a course of action for an addiction.

rational person when she started going to Al-Anon. She wasn't angry any more. I wanted that for myself."

How does Doug feel about alcohol? "I don't think it's a bad thing," he said, "but it probably won't be good for me. I have a lot of traits that alcoholics have. Like when I enjoy something, I always want more of it. I won't decide until I'm twenty-one anyway."[1]

Why People Drink Alcohol

A 2011 Gallup poll found that 64 percent of people in the United States drink alcohol. Right now, you may be asking yourself, if alcohol is bad for you, why do so many people drink in the first place? You've already learned the main reason—to socialize. You've even discovered that drinking moderately is okay. Now let's look at some of the other reasons both adults and young people drink:

Social or Peer Pressure: Some people drink just because others are drinking. They worry that their friends will judge them as unsociable or not "with it" if they don't join the crowd. Peer pressure doesn't just happen among young people. Many adults also worry about the opinions of others. When they follow the example of their friends who drink too much, however, it can lead to problems.

Stress: Work, school, finances, health, and family and personal relationships can all cause stress. Drinking alcohol can help people take their minds off their worries—but only for a while. It may give them a worse problem in the end.

Emotional Problems: Anger, depression, anxiety, and boredom can all trigger drinking in some people. They use alcohol to escape their problems, but it only magnifies them instead. An angry person who drinks becomes angrier, as we saw with Doug's father. A depressed person becomes more depressed. The only way out is to get professional help.

Inhibition: People who are awkward or shy in social situations may drink to feel more comfortable. Drinking alcohol helps to relax them and makes them appear more outgoing. Their confidence only lasts as long as the drinking, however. A better solution would be to learn how to overcome their shyness.

Loneliness: People can feel lonely even when they are surrounded by others. Maybe they've moved to a new place or they don't have enough self-esteem to believe that anyone would want to know them. Sometimes divorce or the death of a loved one can make people feel lonely. Whatever the reason, it's tempting for some people to hide their feelings by drinking alcohol.

A Closer Look at Why Young People Drink

According to a national government survey on drug use and health, 10 percent of young people start to experiment with alcohol at age twelve. By age fifteen, approximately 50 percent have had at least one drink. By age eighteen, the number rises to a whopping 70 percent.[3] Teens don't usually drink as often as adults, but when they do drink, they drink more. Besides the reasons already mentioned, why do young people drink in particular?

- They want to imitate their parents' behavior.

- They have access to alcohol at home.

- They tend not to worry about consequences.

- They want to feel or act older.

- They want to be popular.

- They don't want to be made fun of.

- They don't know how to avoid a specific situation.

The last four reasons usually involve peer pressure—a major issue for some young people—so let's take a closer look at it. A peer is someone from your own age group or grade. Peer pressure occurs when someone in your class

• •

It is OK to say no to a drink, even when everyone else is drinking! It might be helpful to practice how to say no before you go to a party. It gives you more confidence when you know what you are going to say.

Social pressure can cause someone to drink just because others are drinking.

• •

or age group "pushes" or "pressures" you into making a choice, whether it's good or bad.

Everyone gives in to peer pressure at one time or another. If you end up doing something good, such as trying out for a sport you enjoy, you might be happy your friend talked you into it. But if you end up doing something wrong or illegal, such as drinking alcohol, you may be angry at yourself for giving in.

How can you learn to say "no" to alcohol, when there's so much pressure to say "yes" to it? What can you do when someone makes fun of you, puts you down, threatens to reject you if you don't have a drink, or even tries to convince you that drinking is okay?

Saying "no" isn't easy for anyone. You can avoid the situation in the first place by hanging out with friends who make smart choices and avoid alcohol. That shouldn't be too hard. Contrary to popular opinion, most young people don't drink as much as their peers think they do.

It's always good to be prepared with an "out," though. You might say, "My coach will drop me from the team if I get caught drinking," or "Sorry, I have a dentist appointment today," or "My parents would ground me for life." Make sure you decide on your excuse ahead of time, and practice it with a friend you trust. Many school prevention programs include workshops where kids can practice ways to say "no."

Someone may still make fun of you, but who needs a friend like that? Always remember that you have the right to make your own choices, in spite of what someone else says. You're the one who has to live with your choices and the consequences of your actions, not the person who's pressuring you.

It's a Family Problem

It should be clear by now that alcoholics aren't the only people affected by their drinking. Their friends and families suffer the consequences, too. In fact, alcoholism is often referred to as "the family disease."

Parents who have a problem with drinking can affect a family in a number of ways. They may have trouble holding down a job or paying the bills. The money they spend on alcohol may deprive the family of basic needs. They may abuse their children physically and emotionally or neglect them by not giving them enough care. Alcoholic parents can be unpredictable, make promises they don't keep, fight with each other, and even endanger their kids by driving impaired.

Children of alcoholics are often at greater risk of emotional problems because they can't go to their own parents for support. Children may be angry, depressed, confused, embarrassed, guilty, anxious, or all of the above.

They may also feel responsible for their parents' drinking and angry about it at the same time. They worry about their parents, but they feel helpless to change things. Not knowing what to expect from their parents, they may walk around on eggshells, or avoid inviting friends over because they're ashamed of their parents' behavior.

Children of alcoholics often believe that they're alone, that no one else understands how they feel. But they're not alone. A 2012 report showed that an estimated 7.5 million children under the age of eighteen lived in a home with at least one parent who had abused alcohol in the past year.[4] Growing up with an alcoholic parent isn't easy, but knowing there are other kids who share your problem can open the door to healing.

When a Friend Has the Problem

You know or suspect that one of your friends has a drinking problem. How do you handle it? Talking to her when she's been drinking is not a good idea. Better to wait until the next day, when her head is clear again. Lectures and confrontations also don't work. No one likes to be blamed or criticized.

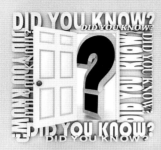

HOW TO COPE WITH PARENTS
Who Have a Drinking Problem

What do you do if your mom or your dad abuse alcohol on a regular basis? If you or a friend are in this situation, there are steps you can take to help.

1. Admit there's a problem. Many alcoholics try to hide their addiction from the outside world. Children often pick up on that need for secrecy. Admitting the truth about a parent's problem is the first step to getting help for yourself.

2. Talk with someone you trust. Share your feelings with a friend, relative, teacher, counselor, or minister. If you don't get support from the first person you talk to, try someone else. Don't give up until you've found the right person who can help.

3. Be tuned into your emotions. You're probably feeling sad, afraid, and confused. Who wouldn't be? You love your parents, but you don't love what they're doing to your family. Write down your feelings so that you can identify them better.

4. Don't try to fix it. Know that you're not to blame for your parents' problem with alcohol and that there's nothing you can do to cure them. Alcoholics need to help themselves.

5. Be safe. Avoid riding in a car with an adult who has been drinking. If your situation at home becomes unsafe, call the National Domestic Violence Hotline at (800) 799-SAFE.

6. Don't assume it will happen to you. Addiction to alcohol does run in families, but that doesn't mean you'll become an alcoholic. Most children of alcoholics don't. As long as you avoid alcohol and make healthy choices for yourself, you'll be able to break the cycle.

7. Join a support group. There are a number of confidential support groups in schools, churches, and neighborhoods that will teach you the skills you need to cope with your situation. You'll also meet other young people who may be struggling with the same issues as you.[5]

You've learned by now that many young people drink because of stress, emotional problems, and insecurity. If you focus on your friend's pain and tell her how you feel about what she's going through, she might be more open to listening to you. You might also talk about the ways her drinking is hurting her and the people around her.

Don't be surprised if your friend gets angry. Denial is a common symptom of alcohol abuse. After she calms down and takes time to think about it, she may take your comments to heart. At worst, you've planted a seed. Once your friend is ready to get help, be prepared to show her how to get it.[6] The following section will give you some ideas on how to do that.

When You Have the Problem

Getting over a drinking problem isn't easy. In fact, people who are alcoholics have to work at staying sober for the rest of their lives. The right treatment, though, can make recovery easier and more successful.

Admitting you have a drinking problem is the first, and most difficult, step. In fact, denial is one of the biggest obstacles to getting help. If you've managed to overcome that hurdle, the next step is to tell your parents or an adult you can trust. They can get the information you need to help you recover.

Depending on the degree of your abuse or dependency, you may need to go through detox, or detoxification. During this process, your body clears itself of alcohol. Detox should be managed by a medical professional who can give you drugs to get through safely. At present, there are three

Overwhelming work at the office can cause stress. Some people drink alcohol to cope with their stress, but it is only a short-term effect.

drugs used for alcohol withdrawal. One decreases a craving for alcohol, another reduces withdrawal symptoms, and a third may cause nausea if you drink alcohol.

Now the serious work begins: a treatment program. In a long-term residential program you might live in a treatment community for six to twelve months. In an outpatient program, you can live at home, even stay in school, and go for treatment on a regular basis. Individual and group counseling are usually included in both types of program. Twelve-step programs like AA are best used as support both during and after treatment.

What's the right kind of treatment for you? Scientific studies show that programs using Cognitive Behavioral Therapy (CBT) work well, especially when positive reinforcement is included. CBT focuses on changing a person's faulty thinking in order to change his behavior. With CBT, patients practice skills to help them resist alcohol. They also work on improving personal relationships and replacing drinking with more rewarding activities. Still, alcohol abuse is often complicated by other factors. There's no "one size fits all" treatment.

Several treatments have been developed just for teens. They focus on the influence of family, peers, and the community in a young person's life. In these programs, teens learn to communicate their thoughts and feelings better, while parents learn to have a more positive influence on their children. You can learn more about how to find the right treatment from the National Institute on Drug Abuse (NIDA). Information about NIDA can be found in For More Information at the back of the book.[7]

One more thing: When you stop drinking, you need to change other habits, too. Hanging out with people who drink and going to places where alcohol is served can be dangerous. On the other hand, finding new friends and new activities that don't involve alcohol can help. Healthy habits, like eating right, getting enough sleep, and exercising can also help you stay strong and recover.

Recovering from alcohol abuse or alcoholism isn't easy. Many people relapse—go back to drinking—several times before finally quitting for good. But with time, courage, and lots of support from friends, family, and substance abuse professionals, recovery is possible.

Chapter 6

What's Up *Next?*

Kayla* has blocked out most of her childhood. Her alcoholic father, who was also a drug addict, left when she was four months old. Her mother, who's been married four times, is an alcoholic. The few memories Kayla has include a lot of abuse, both verbal and physical.

"My mother always told me what a bad kid I was, how she didn't want me around, that my A's weren't good enough," said Kayla. "Some of the people she allowed into my life abused me, too."

Kayla is now nineteen. She describes her mother as a functioning alcoholic. She was able to work, "but as soon as she got home she'd start drinking and, after a while, she would pass out."

* Not her real name

Sometimes her mom invaded her room in the middle of the night to scream at her. "I was so afraid that I would sleep in the closet to prepare myself for dealing with her abuse. My hands even had marks from clenching them so tight every night."

Kayla had her first drink when she was in seventh grade and got drunk for the first time in eighth grade. "I was in pain and I knew from other people how to get out of pain," she explained. When the alcohol didn't provide enough relief at first, she drank more and more. "It put me to sleep. It didn't hurt when I slept."

Kayla continued to numb herself with alcohol throughout high school. She was intelligent enough to get good grades, but she had to conceal her drinking. "I was sneaky," she said. "I hid alcohol with my books in friends' lockers so I wouldn't get caught." Her drinking eventually led to drugs, but she doesn't remember which drugs she used. She was always drunk when she took them. "I'm not proud of what I did," Kayla admitted.

Kayla believed that her life was normal, not realizing that her mother had a serious alcohol problem. She thought her mother was just a bitter, unhappy person who didn't want to deal with her life. One day, she phoned her grand-mother to complain about her mother's abuse. Her grand-mother told Kayla that her mother was a hopeless alcoholic. Nobody had used that word to describe her mom before.

Kayla began to question her own use of alcohol. She had started arriving late at work, or feeling hungover, and she worried about losing her job. She thought if she could get her mother to quit drinking, maybe she could quit, too. But

Kayla soon realized that she had to take responsibility for herself first. Still, she was positive she wasn't an alcoholic.

Then fate stepped in, and she met a woman who brought her to an AA meeting. "These people are talking about me," she recalled thinking. "How do they know so much about me?" It took Kayla a few months to admit she needed to get

THE COST OF Underage Drinking

There are many costs to society from alcohol abuse, especially to young people who drink. Over the years, scientists have studied the consequences of underage drinking. Here is some of what they've learned. Children who drink alcohol are more likely than nondrinkers:

- To get bad grades and have poor performance in school.
- To make bad decisions or do something they'll regret when they're sober.
- To have health issues, like depression and anxiety disorders.
- To be sexually active earlier, have sex more often, and have unprotected sex.
- To use drugs, such as marijuana and cocaine.
- To suffer death or injury from crimes, including rape, robbery, burglary, and car theft.

Any one of these consequences could change the course of a young person's life – and the life of those around him.[3]

sober, but she finally did. "It really sucks when you find out you're an alcoholic. It scared the crap out of me."

Kayla now attends several AA and Al-Anon meetings every week and has a mentor she genuinely admires. "We have a lot in common," she said. "She is who I want to be." She calls her AA sponsor "Mom" and sees her as the mother she never had.

Kayla no longer associates with her old drinking friends. She moved out of her mother's house and is living with another friend and her family. "I have my own bed, a bureau, and a closet I don't have to sleep in," she said.

"AA saved my life," said Kayla, who is grateful for her new friends. "They're my family now." She is working on seeing herself in a positive way. "A few months ago, a friend in AA said 'I love you' to me," she shared. They were words she'd never heard from her mother. Her new friends tell Kayla they love her every day as she continues her recovery.[1]

The Price We Pay

There's no doubt that alcohol can benefit society, at least for those who can enjoy it wisely. But alcohol can have a destructive side. Kayla paid a high price for her mother's excessive drinking – a lost childhood, endless abuse, lack of self-esteem, and her own journey into alcoholism. Multiply Kayla by the millions of people who either drink excessively or live with someone who does, and you end up with a huge cost to families, communities, and society in general.

Let's look at the statistics. In 2011, the Centers for Disease Control and Prevention (CDC) reported that the cost of alcoholism and alcohol abuse in the United States

If you know someone has been drinking and should not drive, call a cab to take them home.

• •

had reached almost $224 billion in 2006 (the latest year information was available). That adds up to $746 per person!

The greatest cost? Loss of wages, which meant lower household incomes for excessive drinkers and their families. Other expenses were for healthcare, law enforcement, and motor vehicle accidents. Also, the CDC reported in 2012 that alcohol abuse was responsible for 82,000 deaths in the

United States each year. That doesn't include the emotional cost to people like Kayla.

The loss of wages and other expenses came primarily as a result of binge drinking. As the CDC director Dr. Thomas Friedan put it, "binge drinking means binge spending."[2]

What Can Be Done?

The CDC suggests ways to discourage people from drinking illegally or excessively. They are called interventions because they "intervene" with alcohol abuse to prevent harm. Here are a few examples:

1. Increasing taxes on alcohol to make it less affordable for young people and frequent drinkers.

2. Holding owners of places that sell alcohol legally responsible for injuries inflicted by customers, such as an auto accident.

3. Lowering BAC levels for younger, less experienced drivers.

4. Enforcing laws that prohibit the sale of alcohol to minors through "sting operations" and more frequent checks.

5. Launching mass media campaigns to warn adults and young people about the dangers of drinking and driving.

Knowledge Is Power

Kids are smart today, but they're often in the dark when it comes to the realities of alcohol use and abuse. Even

Even the smartest teens need information about how alcohol abuse impacts their family. It is important for them to find a trusted adult or professional to talk to.

young people who have alcoholics in their families may not understand the impact it has on them.

Back in the 1500s, a scientist by the name of Francis Bacon wrote, "Knowledge is power." In other words, understanding a problem is the first step in knowing how to deal with it. Young people who are aware of the dangers of alcohol are able to make smart choices about whether to use it—or not.

Research on preventing alcohol abuse is growing every day. Schools, families, and communities are putting effective programs into practice.

School-based prevention programs once used scare tactics to get kids to avoid alcohol. Alcohol abuse is scary, but the newer programs are better. They discuss the social pressure on young people to drink and give them the tools to resist it.

Home-based prevention programs also make a difference. Why? Parents have a huge influence on their children, whether or not kids want to admit it. These programs teach parents how to set rules about drinking, enforce those rules, and keep an eye on their kids' behavior. Put into action, these programs may actually reduce the odds of young people drinking.

Community-based prevention programs are essential to make people aware of the frequency of underage drinking. Once again, knowledge is power. Together, community organizations can work with schools and families to make kids more aware of the dangers of alcohol abuse.[4]

The Internet also plays an important role in teaching young people about alcohol. What kid today doesn't know

more about finding information online than his or her parents? Luckily, there are a number of user-friendly Web sites that young people can access to learn more about alcohol. For their Web addresses go to For More Information at the back of the book.

It's a Shame . . . Isn't It?

Up until now, only a small percentage of problem drinkers have used the programs and treatments available to help them recover. Two reasons for that may be:

Shame: The belief that drinking excessively is a weakness is still strong in our society. Many problem drinkers worry they'll be judged if people know how much they drink. They try to hide their problems from the rest of the world—sometimes until it's too late.

Lack of Awareness: Many alcoholics and abusers know about AA and other twelve-step programs. But they aren't aware that more effective programs may be available. Some have no insurance and believe that they can't afford to get help. Others have problems keeping appointments.

Researchers agree that broadening the reach of treatment is essential. Doctors are being trained to screen, diagnose, and treat patients during routine healthcare visits in offices, clinics, and emergency rooms. They're also learning to prescribe medicines that treat alcohol problems. Keeping contact with patients is the key to helping them.

Since many new patients drop out of programs too soon, researchers are searching for ways to make staying in treatment more tempting. New programs offer user-friendly services, such as parking, child care, and convenient appointments. Although lack of insurance is still a problem, new legislation has been enacted to ensure that people will be able to afford the treatment they need. For instance, the new Affordable Care Act requires insurance companies to cover treatment for addiction to alcohol as a chronic disease.

The Internet is becoming an important factor in treating alcohol abuse, too. Patients can get treatment there twenty-four hours a day, seven days a week. They can take tests to see how severe their problem is, find exercises to set goals, and learn techniques to prevent relapse. One program uses smartphone apps to give individual patients information, strategies, reminders, and support.[5]

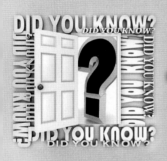

A PILL THAT WILL LET *People Drink— Moderately*

Researchers are just beginning to study the medical reasons why people begin to drink and why they can't stop. In fact, about 90 percent of alcoholics experience at least one relapse over a four-year period after treatment. Some scientists believe that the ability to manage drinking occurs in the frontal lobe of the brain, the area in charge of self-control. Long term drug therapy combined with counseling may be the answer. One study is testing a pill that will someday allow some alcoholics to have an occasional drink yet control the desire to drink too much.[6]

It All Adds Up

Knowledge, prevention, treatment. Alcohol can be an instrument of pleasure or destruction. Whether you choose to drink alcohol in the future or not, the first step is to know what it's all about. The next step is to make educated choices about its use. Even the smartest adults can kid themselves about their drinking habits. The final step is to get involved in helping to manage alcohol abuse by educating others. Young people can make a difference.

• •

Instead of drinking, get involved doing fun, creative, and safe activities with friends.

Chapter Notes

Chapter 1

ALCOHOL, Seriously

1. Stephen King, *On Writing* (New York: Scribners, 2000), Kindle e-book (June 23, 2012).
2. Mark Wallace, "Stephen King's Alcoholism and Drug Addiction in the 70s and 80s," February 22, 2011, Suite 101, <http://suite101.com/article/stephen-kings-alcohol> (June 23, 2012).
3. PubMed Health, U.S. National Library of Medicine, "Alcoholism and Alcohol Abuse," <www.ncbi.nlm.nih.gov/pubmedhealth/PMH0001940/> (August 4, 2012).
4. Centers for Disease Control and Prevention, "Frequently Asked Questions – Alcohol," <www.cdc.gov/alcohol/faqs.htm> (May 25, 2013).
5. National Institute on Alcohol Abuse and Alcoholism, "Underage Drinking," <www.niaaa.nih.gov/alcohol-health/special-populations-co-occurring-disorders/underage-drinking> (June 23, 2012).
6. National Institute on Alcohol Abuse and Alcoholism, "College Drinking," <www.niaaa.nih.gov/alcohol-health/special-populations-co-occurring-disorders/college- drinking> (June 23, 2012).
7. National Highway Traffic Safety Administration, "Driver Education," <www.nhtsa.gov/Driving+Safety/Driver+Education> (August 8, 2012).

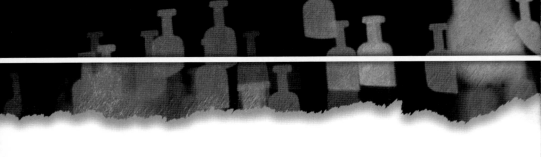

Chapter 2

ALCOHOL
Through the Ages

1. David J. Hanson, Ph.D., "Alcohol Problems and Solutions—History of Alcohol and Drinking around the World," adapted from David J. Hanson, *Preventing Alcohol Abuse: Alcohol, Culture and Control*, (Westport, Conn.: Praeger, 1995), <http://www2.potsdam.edu/hansondj/controversies/1114796842.html> (May 29, 2012).
2. Ibid.

Chapter 3

HOW ALCOHOL
Works

1. Michael R. Shea, "Huge Amount of Alcohol Killed Teen, Coroner Says," *The Modesto Bee*, March 20, 2008, <www.modbee.com/2008/03/20/244848> (July 10, 2012).
2. Michael R. Shea, "Vigil Held in Wake of Teen's Mysterious Death," *The Modesto Bee*, January 3, 2008, <http://www.modbee.com/2008/01/03/168742.> (July 10, 2012).
3. Centers for Disease Control and Prevention, "CDC reports excessive alcohol consumption cost the U.S. $224 billion in 2006," October 17, 2011, <http://www.cdc.gov/media/releases/2011/p1017_alcohol_consumption.html> (August 27, 2012).

Chapter 4 — ALCOHOL'S *Uncool Aftereffects*

1. Authors' personal interview with "Tyler," August 26, 2012.
2. National Highway Traffic Safety Administration, "Impaired Driving," <www.nhtsa.gov/Impaired> (August 15, 2012).
3. FindLaw, "DUI Checkpoints," <http://dui.findlaw.com/dui-arrests/dui-checkpoints.html> (August, 22, 2012).

Chapter 5 — DEALING WITH ALCOHOL *in Everyday Life*

1. Authors' phone interview with "Doug" and "Linda," August 13, 2012.
2. Carole Bennett, MA, "From Heartache to Hope: Life with the Alcoholic/Addict—Is there a 'Dry Drunk' in your life?" *Psychology Today*, May 14, 2011, <http://www.psychologytoday.com/blog/heartache-hope/201105/is-there-dry-drunk-in-your-life> (August 14, 2012).
3. Center for Substance Abuse Prevention, Too Smart to Start, Families, "Underage Drinking Statistics," (May 14, 2012). <http://www.toosmarttostart.samhsa.gov/families/facts/statistics.aspx> (August 15, 2012).
4. Substance Abuse & Mental Health Services Administration, SAMHSA News Release "Report shows 7.5 million children live with a parent with an alcohol use disorder," February 16, 2012, <http://www.samhsa.gov/newsroom/advisories/1202151415.aspx> (August, 26, 2012).

5. TeensHealth.org, "Coping with an Alcoholic Parent," (reviewed by Michelle J. New, Ph.D., February 2010), <http://kidshealth. org/teen/your_mind/families/coping_alcoholic.html> (August 13, 2012).

6. Hazelden, "How to Talk with a Friend with a Drinking Problem," <http://www.hazelden.org/web/public/has90412. page> (June 9, 2013)

7. National Institute on Drug Abuse (NIDA), *Principles of Drug Addiction Treatment: A Research-Based Guide* (Third Edition), December 2012, <http://www.drugabuse.gov/publications/ principles-drug-addiction-treatment> (June 9, 2013)

Chapter 6

1. Authors' phone interview with "Kayla," August 23, 2012.

2. Centers for Disease Control and Prevention, "CDC reports excessive alcohol consumption cost the U.S. $224 billion in 2006," October 17, 2011, <http://www.cdc.gov./media/ releases/2011/p1017_alcohol_consumption.html> (August 27, 2012).

3. Substance Abuse and Mental Health Services Administration (SAMHSA), "The Consequences of Underage Drinking," Underage Drinking Prevention National Campaign, <http:// www.samhsa.gov/underagedrinking/tabresources/tab1/ Consequences-of Underage.pdf> (May 15, 2013)

4. National Institute on Drug Abuse (NIDA), "Preventing Drug Abuse among Children and Adolescents (In Brief): Prevention Principles," <http://www.drugabuse.gov/publications/ preventing-drug-abuse-among-children-adolescents/ prevention-principles. (June 1, 2013)

5. National Institute on Alcohol Abuse and Alcoholism, "Alcohol Alert, No. 81—Exploring Treatment Options for Alcohol Use Disorders," 2011, <http://pubs.niaaa.nih.gov/publications/AA81/AA81.htm> (August 28, 2012).

6. Susan Seligson, "Dry—A new treatment for alcoholism defies the recovery movement," *Bostonia*, Fall 2010 <http://www.bu.edu/bostonia/fall10/dry/> (August, 28, 2010).

Glossary

addiction—A constant, uncontrollable need for a substance, even though the user knows it's harmful.

Al-Anon—An organized group of families and friends of alcoholics who aren't alcoholics themselves. They meet on a regular basis to share their experiences and give each other help and support.

alcohol—A colorless liquid, produced when yeast, sugars, and starches are broken down by a chemical process called fermentation. Alcohol is also a general term meaning any kind of intoxicating drink containing alcohol.

alcohol abuse—Having unhealthy or dangerous drinking habits that can lead to alcohol addiction.

alcohol dependence—A physical disease in which a person drinks heavily over a period of time and can't slow down or stop. Also called alcohol addiction or alcoholism.

alcohol poisoning—A condition in which a large amount of alcohol is consumed, usually in a short amount of time. It can be deadly.

alcoholic—A person who suffers from alcoholism.

Alcoholics Anonymous (AA)—A program that helps alcoholics of all ages get sober and stay sober by holding meetings where people share their experiences and support each other.

binge drinking—Consuming a large amount of alcohol over a short period of time. For men, this equals five or more drinks in a row. For women, it equals four or more drinks in a row.

blood alcohol concentration (BAC)—The amount of alcohol present in a person's blood after drinking. It's also called blood alcohol content or blood alcohol level and is measured as a percentage.

breath alcohol testing instrument—A device often used by the police to determine how much alcohol is in a person's blood. People blow into a tube on the testing device, and it measures the percentage of alcohol in the blood.

chronic disease—A disease that develops slowly over time and lasts years or a lifetime.

cirrhosis—A chronic, life-threatening disease that causes liver cells to be damaged and replaced by scar tissues. It gets worse over time and is often caused by long-term alcoholism.

cognitive behavioral therapy—a therapy that focuses on changing a person's faulty thinking in order to change his behavior.

coma—A deep, unconscious state. It has many causes, including alcohol poisoning.

condensation—The chemical process of changing gas into a liquid. This is one step in making distilled alcohol.

depressant—A substance that slows down brain function and activity.

designated driver—A person who agrees not to drink, or to drink very little, in order to drive others home safely.

detoxification—A medically supervised program that helps people withdraw from alcohol or another abused substance.

distilling—The process used to produce alcoholic spirits. It involves boiling liquid and condensing its vapor.

driving under the influence (DUI)—Operating a motor vehicle with a BAC at 0.08 percent or above.

evaporation—The process in which a liquid is changed to a vapor without its temperature reaching the boiling point. This is one step in making distilled alcohol.

fermentation—The process of using yeast to convert sugar to carbon dioxide and alcohol.

fetal alcohol syndrome—A disorder that causes permanent damage to an unborn baby when pregnant mothers drink alcohol. Children have slow growth, delayed development, and learning disabilities.

field sobriety tests—Tests conducted by the police to determine if a driver is over the legal BAC limit. Drivers must follow orders and perform simple physical tasks.

heavy drinker—On average, a man who drinks more than two drinks a day, and a woman who drinks more than one drink a day.

hops—The dried blossom of the female hop plant, a climbing herb. The seed cones are used to make beer.

interventions—Ways of interfering to improve health, such as discouraging people from drinking illegally or excessively. Some examples are increasing taxes on alcohol and lowering legal BAC levels for younger drivers.

intoxication—Also called drunkenness. This is the state of mental and physical impairment that occurs when someone drinks too much. Intoxication is also measured by BAC levels.

moderate drinker—Generally used to describe a man who has no more than two drinks a day and a woman who has no more than one drink a day.

oxidation—The process of changing alcohol in the body into water, carbon dioxide, and energy by the liver.

pathogen—An agent that causes disease, such as a bacterium or a virus.

peer pressure—Pressure to adopt a type of behavior in order to be accepted as part of a group of friends or classmates.

prevention programs—Programs designed for schools, communities, or homes to teach about alcohol and help prevent its abuse.

Prohibition—A national ban on the sale, manufacture, and transportation of alcohol in the United States from 1920 to 1933.

sobriety checkpoint—Police checkpoints along the road to randomly stop vehicles and check for impaired drivers.

social drinker—A person who drinks in a safe, responsible, legal manner without trying to get drunk.

stroke— The sudden death of brain cells due to inadequate blood flow.

Organizations

Alcoholics Anonymous
A.A. World Services, Inc.
P.O. Box 459
New York, NY 10163
(212) 870-3400
<http://www.aa.org>

Al-Anon/Alateen
Al-Anon Family Group Headquarters
1600 Corporate Landing Parkway
Virginia Beach, VA 23454
(757) 563-1600
<http://www.al-anon.alateen.org/>

Centers for Disease Control and Prevention
1600 Clifton Road
Atlanta, GA 30333
(800) 232- 4636
<http://www.cdc.gov/>

National Highway Traffic Safety Administration
1200 New Jersey Avenue SE, West Building
Washington, DC 20590
(888) 327-4236
<http://www.nhtsa.gov/>

National Institute on Alcohol Abuse and Alcoholism (NIAAA)
Publications Distribution Center
PO Box 10686
Rockville, MD 20849
<http://www.niaaa.nih.gov/>

Secular Organizations for Sobriety (SOS)
4773 Hollywood Boulevard
Hollywood, CA 90027
(323) 666-4295
<http://www.centerforinquiry.net/ sos>

SMART Recovery
7304 Mentor Avenue, Suite F
Mentor, OH 44060
(866) 951-5357
<http://www.smartrecovery.org/>

Books

Aretha, David. *On the Rocks: Teens and Alcohol.* Danbury, Conn.: Children's Press, 2007.

Bellenir, Karen, ed. *Alcohol Information for Teens: Health Tips About Alcohol Use, Abuse, and Dependence.* Detroit, Mich.: Omnigraphics Inc., 2013.

Freidman, Lauri S. *Alcohol.* Farmington Hills, Mich.: Greenhaven Press, 2010.

Gass, Justin T. *Alcohol.* New York: Chelsea House Publications, 2010.

Stewart, Gail. *Drowning in a Bottle: Teens and Alcohol Abuse.* North Mankato, Minn.: Compass Point Books, 2009.

Watkins, Christine. *Alcohol Abuse.* Farmington Hills, Mich.: Greenhaven Press, 2012.

Internet Addresses

National Institute on Alcohol Abuse and Alcoholism (NIAAA). *The Cool Spot.gov.* © 2012
<http://www.thecoolspot.gov/>

Office of National Drug Control Policy. *National Youth Anti-drug Media Campaign. Above the Influence.com* © 2012
<http://www.abovetheinfluence.com/>

Substance Abuse and Mental Health Services Administration (SAMHSA). *Too Smart to Start.* © 2012
<http://www.toosmarttostart.samhsa.gov>

Index

A

acetaldehyde, 41
adaptive stage, 50
Affordable Care Act, 89
Al-Anon, 66, 82
Alateen, 67
alcohol
    addiction, dependence, 14–
        16, 35, 48, 75
    advertising, images, 38–39
    classification, 12
    deaths from, 21–22, 43,
        83–84
    economic costs, 82–84
    effects generally, 12–14, 21,
        41, 42, 45
    families, effects on, 10–11,
        22, 65–68, 72–73
    hangovers, 8, 10
    health effects generally,
        62–64
    motivations to use, 10, 24,
        31, 68–71
    myths, 51–53
    safe amounts of, 14
    statistics, 6, 7, 16, 52, 53, 69,
        73, 82–83
alcohol content, 14, 15, 24, 29
alcohol dehydrogenase, 49
Alcoholics Anonymous, 10, 16,
    66, 77, 81, 82
alcoholism, 14, 16, 35, 49–51, 53,
    60–62
alcohol poisoning, 36–38, 41
alcohol tolerance, 53

alcohol withdrawal, 16, 75, 77
alembic, 29
Arabs, 29
Asians, Asian flush, 49, 52

B

beer, 24–26, 28
beer belly, 53
binge drinking, 21, 37, 41, 52, 63,
    84
Black Death, 29
blood alcohol concentration
    (BAC), 36, 42, 43, 57
bootleggers, 34
brain changes, 21, 51, 89
brandy, 29
Breathalyzer, 55, 60
Buddhists, 35

C

checkpoints, 59
child abuse, 47, 79–80
children of alcoholics, 65–68,
    72–74, 79–82
China, 24
Christian Church, 27
cognitive behavioral therapy
    (CBT), 77
college students, 21
coma, 43
condensation, 29
confusion, 43
coping strategies, 71–72, 74
cultural factors, 47

D

death, 21–22, 43, 83–84
delirium tremens, 51
dependence stage alcoholism, 50
designated driver, 44
detox, 16, 75, 77
distillation, 29–31
Doug, 65–68
drinking patterns, 46
driving, 44, 57–60
dry drunk, 67
DUI, 57, 58

E

education, 84–88
Egyptians, 24–26, 28
Eighteenth Amendment, 33
endstage alcoholism, 50–51
ethanol, 12
ethnic groups, 49, 52
euphoria, 42
Europeans, 26–27, 49
evaporation, 29
excitement, 43

F

family history, 46, 72–73
fermentation, 23–24
fetal alcohol syndrome, 63, 64
Ford, Betty, 18
Fox, Michael J., 18

G

gender, 46
genes, 46, 49, 53
gin, 31

Gonzalez, Julia, 36–38, 41
Grant, Ulysses S., 18
Greeks, 26–27

H

heavy drinking defined, 14
history
    colonial America, 31
    fermentation, 23–24
    medicinal uses, 24, 31, 35
    Prohibition, 33, 34
    uses of alcohol generally, 24,
      26, 27, 29, 31
hops, 28

I

India, 24
inhibition, 69
insurance, 88, 89
interventions, 10–11, 73–75, 84

K

Kayla, 79–82, 84
King, Stephen, 8–11
King, Tabitha, 10

L

Linda, 65–68
liver, 39–40, 62
liver disease, 62
loneliness, 69

M

Mantle, Mickey, 18
mead, 26
medicinal uses, 24, 26, 31, 35
mental health, 46, 68–69

metabolism of alcohol, 39–42, 49
monasteries, 28
Muslims, 35

N
National Domestic Violence Hotline, 74
Native Americans, 49, 52

O
open containers, 59
oxidation, 39–41

P
pathogens, 24
peer pressure, 68–71
Poe, Edgar Allen, 18
pregnancy, 14, 63, 64
prevention, 71–72, 84–88
problem drinking, 16, 44–47, 73–75
Prohibition, 33, 34
punishments, penalties, 27, 31, 54–60, 62

R
responsible drinking, 43–44
Romans, 27
Rush, Benjamin, 33, 35
Rutgers Alcohol Problem Index, 61

S
Sarah, 54–57
saying no, 71–72
sobriety tests, 55, 59–60
social factors, 46, 68–71

speakeasies, 34
stages of intoxication, 42–43
standards, 14
straws, 28
stress, 68
stupor, 43
Sumerians, 24, 28
support groups, 16, 66–68, 74, 81, 82
Sura, 24

T
teens, young people, 14, 16–21, 44, 54–57, 61, 69–71, 72, 77
temperance movement, 33
treatment, 16, 50–51, 75, 77–78, 88–89
twelve-step programs, 67, 77
Tyler, 54–57

U
underage drinking, 16–22, 54–57, 62, 80, 81, 82
Urban, Keith, 18

V
vomiting, 41

Y
Water of Life, 28–31
wine, 24, 26–28, 43–44, 53
Winehouse, Amy, 18